AGAMEMNON

AESCHYLUS

ISBN: 978-1502375490

AGAMEMNON

CHARACTERS IN THE PLAY

A WATCHMAN
CHORUS OF ARGIVE ELDERS
CLYTEMNESTRA, wife of AGAMEMNON
A HERALD
AGAMEMNON, King of Argos
CASSANDRA, daughter of Priam, and slave of AGAMEMNON
AEGISTHUS, son of Thyestes, cousin of AGAMEMNON
Servants, Attendants, Soldiers

(SCENE:-Before the palace of AGAMEMNON in Argos. In front of
the palace there are statues of the gods, and altars prepared for
sacrifice. It is night. On the roof of the palace can be
discerned a WATCHMAN.)

*

A Watchman:

I pray the gods to quit me of my toils,
To close the watch I keep, this livelong year;
For as a watch-dog lying, not at rest,
Propped on one arm, upon the palace-roof
Of Atreus' race, too long, too well I know
The starry conclave of the midnight sky,
Too well, the splendours of the firmament,
The lords of light, whose kingly aspect shows--
What time they set or climb the sky in turn--
The year's divisions, bringing frost or fire.

And now, as ever, am I set to mark
When shall stream up the glow of signal-flame,
The bale-fire bright, and tell its Trojan tale--
"Troy town is ta'en:" such issue holds in hope
She in whose woman's breast beats heart of man.

Thus upon mine unrestful couch I lie,
Bathed with the dews of night, unvisited
By dreams--ah me!--for in the place of sleep
Stands Fear as my familiar, and repels
The soft repose that would mine eyelids seal.
And if at whiles, for the lost balm of sleep,
I medicine my soul with melody
Of trill or song--anon to tears I turn,
Wailing the woe that broods upon this home,
Not now by honour guided as of old.

But now at last fair fall the welcome hour
That sets me free, whene'er the thick night glow
With beacon-fire of hope deferred no more.
All hail!

A beacon-light is seen reddening the distant sky.

Fire of the night, that brings my spirit day,
Shedding on Argos light, and dance, and song,
Greetings to fortune, hail!

Let my loud summons ring within the ears
Of Agamemnon's queen, that she anon
Start from her couch and with a shrill voice cry
A joyous welcome to the beacon-blaze,
For Ilion's fall; such fiery message gleams
From yon high flame; and I, before the rest,
Will foot the lightsome measure of our joy;
For I can say, "My master's dice fell fair--
Behold! the triple sice, the lucky flame!"
Now be my lot to clasp, in loyal love,
The hand of him restored, who rules our home:
Home--but I say no more: upon my tongue
Treads hard the ox o' the adage.
Had it voice,
The home itself might soothliest tell its tale;
I, of set will, speak words the wise may learn,
To others, nought remember nor discern.

Exit. The chorus of old men of Mycenae enter, each leaning on a staff. During their song Clytemnestra appears in the background, kindling the altars.

Chorus:

Ten livelong years have rolled away,
Since the twin lords of sceptred sway,
By Zeus endowed with pride of place,
The doughty chiefs of Atreus' race,
Went forth of yore,
To plead with Priam, face to face,
Before the judgment-seat of War!

A thousand ships from Argive land
Put forth to bear the martial band,
That with a spirit stern and strong
Went out to right the kingdom's wrong--
Pealed, as they went, the battle-song,
Wild as the vultures' cry;
When o'er the eyrie, soaring high,
In wild bereavèd agony,
Around, around, in airy rings,
They wheel with oarage of their wings,
But not the eyas-brood behold,
That called them to the nest of old;
But let Apollo from the sky,
Or Pan, or Zeus, but hear the cry,
The exile cry, the wail forlorn,
Of birds from whom their home is torn--
On those who wrought the rapine fell,
Heaven sends the vengeful fiends of hell.

Even so doth Zeus, the jealous lord
And guardian of the hearth and board,
Speed Atreus' sons, in vengeful ire,
'Gainst Paris--sends them forth on fire,
Her to buy back, in war and blood,

Whom one did wed but many woo'd!
And many, many, by his will,
The last embrace of foes shall feel,
And many a knee in dust be bowed,
And splintered spears on shields ring loud,
Of Trojan and of Greek, before
That iron bridal-feast be o'er!
But as he willed 'tis ordered all,
And woes, by heaven ordained, must fall--
Unsoothed by tears or spilth of wine
Poured forth too late, the wrath divine
Glares vengeance on the flameless shrine.

And we in gray dishonoured eld,
Feeble of frame, unfit were held
To join the warrior array
That then went forth unto the fray:
And here at home we tarry, fain
Our feeble footsteps to sustain,
Each on his staff--so strength doth wane,
And turns to childishness again.
For while the sap of youth is green,
And, yet unripened, leaps within,
The young are weakly as the old,
And each alike unmeet to hold
The vantage post of war!
And ah! when flower and fruit are o'er,
And on life's tree the leaves are sere,
Age wendeth propped its journey drear,
As forceless as a child, as light
And fleeting as a dream of night
Lost in the garish day!

But thou, O child of Tyndareus,
Queen Clytemnestra, speak! and say
What messenger of joy to-day
Hath won thine ear? what welcome news,
That thus in sacrificial wise
E'en to the city's boundaries

Thou biddest altar-fires arise?
Each god who doth our city guard,
And keeps o'er Argos watch and ward
From heaven above, from earth below--
The mighty lords who rule the skies,
The market's lesser deities,
To each and all the altars glow,
Piled for the sacrifice!
And here and there, anear, afar,
Streams skyward many a beacon-star,
Conjur'd and charm'd and kindled well
By pure oil's soft and guileless spell,
Hid now no more
Within the palace' secret store.

O queen, we pray thee, whatsoe'er,
Known unto thee, were well revealed,
That thou wilt trust it to our ear,
And bid our anxious heart be healed!
That waneth now unto despair--
Now, waxing to a presage fair,
Dawns, from the altar, Hope--to scare
From our rent hearts the vulture Care.

List! for the power is mine, to chant on high
The chiefs' emprise, the strength that omens gave!
List! on my soul breathes yet a harmony,
From realms of ageless powers, and strong to save!

How brother kings, twin lords of one command,
Led forth the youth of Hellas in their flower,
Urged on their way, with vengeful spear and brand,
By warrior-birds, that watched the parting hour.

"Go forth to Troy", the eagles seemed to cry--
And the sea-kings obeyed the sky-kings' word,
When on the right they soared across the sky,
And one was black, one bore a white tail barred.

High o'er the palace were they seen to soar,
Then lit in sight of all, and rent and tare,
Far from the fields that she should range no more,
Big with her unborn brood, a mother-hare.

And one beheld, the soldier-prophet true,
And the two chiefs, unlike of soul and will,
In the twy-coloured eagles straight he knew,
And spake the omen forth, for good and ill.

(Ah woe and well-a-day! but be the issue fair!)

"Go forth," he cried, "and Priam's town shall fall.
Yet long the time shall be; and flock and herd,
The people's wealth, that roam before the wall,
Shall force hew down, when Fate shall give the word.

But O beware! lest wrath in Heaven abide,
To dim the glowing battle-forge once more,
And mar the mighty curb of Trojan pride,
The steel of vengeance, welded as for war!

For virgin Artemis bears jealous hate
Against the royal house, the eagle-pair,
Who rend the unborn brood, insatiate--
Yea, loathes their banquet on the quivering hare."

(Ah woe and well-a-day! but be the issue fair!)

"For well she loves--the goddess kind and mild--
The tender new-born cubs of lions bold,
Too weak to range--and well the sucking child
Of every beast that roams by wood and wold.

So to the Lord of Heaven she prayeth still,
"Nay. if it must be, be the omen true!
Yet do the visioned eagles presage ill;
The end be well, but crossed with evil too!"

Healer Apollo! be her wrath controll'd,
Nor weave the long delay of thwarting gales,
To war against the Danaans and withhold
From the free ocean-waves their eager sails!

She craves, alas! to see a second life
Shed forth, a curst unhallowed sacrifice--
'Twixt wedded souls, artificer of strife,
And hate that knows not fear, and fell device.

At home there tarries like a lurking snake,
Biding its time, a wrath unreconciled,"
"A wily watcher, passionate to slake,
In blood, resentment for a murdered child."

Such was the mighty warning, pealed of yore--
Amid good tidings, such the word of fear,
What time the fateful eagles hovered o'er
The kings, and Calchas read the omen clear.

(In strains like his, once more,
Sing woe and well-a-day! but be the issue fair!)

Zeus--if to The Unknown
That name of many names seem good--
Zeus, upon Thee I call.
Thro' the mind's every road
I passed, but vain are all,
Save that which names thee Zeus, the Highest One,
Were it but mine to cast away the load,
The weary load, that weighs my spirit down.

He that was Lord of old,
In full-blown pride of place and valour bold,
Hath fallen and is gone, even as an old tale told!
And he that next held sway,
By stronger grasp o'erthrown
Hath pass'd away!
And whoso now shall bid the triumph-chant arise

To Zeus, and Zeus alone,
He shall be found the truly wise.
'Tis Zeus alone who shows the perfect way
Of knowledge: He hath ruled,
Men shall learn wisdom, by affliction schooled.

In visions of the night, like dropping rain,
Descend the many memories of pain
Before the spirit's sight: through tears and dole
Comes wisdom o'er the unwilling soul--
A boon, I wot, of all Divinity,
That holds its sacred throne in strength, above the sky!

And then the elder chief, at whose command
The fleet of Greece was manned,
Cast on the seer no word of hate,
But veered before the sudden breath of Fate--

Ah, weary while! for, ere they put forth sail,
Did every store, each minish'd vessel, fail,
While all the Achaean host
At Aulis anchored lay,
Looking across to Chalics and the coast
Where refluent waters welter, rock, and sway;
And rife with ill delay
From northern Strymon blew the thwarting blast--
Mother of famine fell,
That holds men wand'ring still
Far from the haven where they fain would be!--
And pitiless did waste
Each ship and cable, rotting on the sea,
And, doubling with delay each weary hour,
Withered with hope deferred th' Achaeans' warlike flower.

But when, for bitter storm, a deadlier relief,
And heavier with ill to either chief,
Pleading the ire of Artemis, the seer avowed,
The two Atridae smote their sceptres on the plain,
And, striving hard, could not their tears restrain!

And then the elder monarch spake aloud--
"Ill lot were mine, to disobey!
And ill, to smite my child, my household's love and pride!
To stain with virgin Hood a father's hands, and slay
My daughter, by the altar's side!
Twixt woe and woe I dwell--
I dare not like a recreant fly,
And leave the league of ships, and fail each true ally;
For rightfully they crave, with eager fiery mind,
The virgin's blood, shed forth to lull the adverse wind--
God send the deed be well!"

Thus on his neck he took
Fate's hard compelling yoke;
Then, in the counter-gale of will abhorr'd, accursed,
To recklessness his shifting spirit veered--
Alas! that Frenzy, first of ills and worst,
With evil craft men's souls to sin hath ever stirred!

And so he steeled his heart--ah, well-a-day--
Aiding a war for one false woman's sake,
His child to slay,
And with her spilt blood make
An offering, to speed the ships upon their way!

Lusting for war, the bloody arbiters
Closed heart and ears, and would nor hear nor heed
The girl-voice plead,
"Pity me, Father!" nor her prayers,
Nor tender, virgin years.

So, when the chant of sacrifice was done,
Her father bade the youthful priestly train
Raise her, like some poor kid, above the altar-stone,
From where amid her robes she lay
Sunk all in swoon away--
Bade them, as with the bit that mutely tames the steed,
Her fair lips' speech refrain,
Lest she should speak a curse on Atreus' home and seed,

So, trailing on the earth her robe of saffron dye,
With one last piteous dart from her beseeching eye
Those that should smite she smote--
Fair, silent, as a pictur'd form, but fain
To plead, "Is all forgot?
How oft those halls of old,
Wherein my sire high feast did hold,"
"Rang to the virginal soft strain,
When I, a stainless child,
Sang from pure lips and undefiled,
Sang of my sire, and all
His honoured life, and how on him should fall
Heaven's highest gift and gain!"
And then--but I beheld not, nor can tell,
What further fate befel:
But this is sure, that Calchas' boding strain
Can ne'er be void or vain.
This wage from Justice' hand do sufferers earn,
The future to discern:
And yet--farewell, O secret of To-morrow!
Fore-knowledge is fore-sorrow.
Clear with the clear beams of the morrow's sun,
The future presseth on.
Now, let the house's tale, how dark soe'er,
Find yet an issue fair!--
So prays the loyal, solitary band
That guards the Apian land.

They turn to Clytemnestra, who leaves the altars and comes forward.

O queen, I come in reverence of thy sway--
For, while the ruler's kingly seat is void,
The loyal heart before his consort bends.
Now--be it sure and certain news of good,
Or the fair tidings of a flatt'ring hope,
That bids thee spread the light from shrine to shrine,
I, fain to hear, yet grudge not if thou hide.

Clytemnestra:

As saith the adage, "From the womb of Night
Spring forth, with promise fair, the young child Light."
Ay--fairer even than all hope my news--
By Grecian hands is Priam's city ta'en!

Chorus:

What say'st thou? doubtful heart makes treach'rous ear.

Clytemnestra:

Hear then again, and plainly--Troy is ours!

Chorus:

Thrills thro' my heart such joy as wakens tears.

Clytemnestra:

Ay, thro' those tears thine eye looks loyalty.

Chorus:

But hast thou proof, to make assurance sure?

Clytemnestra:

Go to; I have--unless the god has lied.

Chorus:

Hath some night-vision won thee to belief?

Clytemnestra:

Out on all presage of a slumb'rous soul!

Chorus:

But wert thou cheered by Rumour's wingless word?

Clytemnestra:

Peace--thou dost chide me as a credulous girl.

Chorus:

Say then, how long ago the city fell?

Clytemnestra:

Even in this night that now brings forth the dawn.

Chorus:

Yet who so swift could speed the message here?

Clytemnestra:

From Ida's top Hephaestus, lord of fire,
Sent forth his sign; and on, and ever on,
Beacon to beacon sped the courier-flame.
From Ida to the crag, that Hermes loves,
Of Lemnos; thence unto the steep sublime
Of Athos, throne of Zeus, the broad blaze flared.
Thence, raised aloft to shoot across the sea,
The moving light, rejoicing in its strength,
Sped from the pyre of pine, and urged its way,
In golden glory, like some strange new sun,
Onward, and reached Macistus' watching heights.
There, with no dull delay nor heedless sleep,
The watcher sped the tidings on in turn,
Until the guard upon Messapius' peak
Saw the far flame gleam on Euripus' tide,
And from the high-piled heap of withered furze
Lit the new sign and bade the message on.

Then the strong light, far flown and yet undimmed,
Shot thro' the sky above Asopus' plain,
Bright as the moon, and on Cithaeron's crag
Aroused another watch of flying fire.
And there the sentinels no whit disowned,
But sent redoubled on, the hest of flame--
Swift shot the light, above Gorgopis' bay,
To Aegiplanctus' mount, and bade the peak
Fail not the onward ordinance of fire.
And like a long beard streaming in the wind,
Full-fed with fuel, roared and rose the blaze,
And onward flaring, gleamed above the cape,
Beneath which shimmers the Saronic bay,
And thence leapt light unto Arachne's peak,
The mountain watch that looks upon our town.
Thence to th' Atrides' roof--in lineage fair,
A bright posterity of Ida's fire.
So sped from stage to stage, fulfilled in turn,
Flame after flame, along the course ordained,
And lo! the last to speed upon its way
Sights the end first, and glows unto the goal.
And Troy is ta'en, and by this sign my lord
Tells me the tale, and ye have learned my word.

Chorus:

To heaven, O queen, will I upraise new song:
But, wouldst thou speak once more, I fain would hear
From first to last the marvel of the tale.

Clytemnestra:

Think you--this very morn--the Greeks in Troy,
And loud therein the voice of utter wail!
Within one cup pour vinegar and oil,
And look! unblent, unreconciled, they war.
So in the twofold issue of the strife
Mingle the victor's shout, the captives' moan.
For all the conquered whom the sword has spared

Cling weeping--some unto a brother slain,
Some childlike to a nursing father's form,
And wail the loved and lost, the while their neck
Bows down already 'neath the captive's chain.
And lo! the victors, now the fight is done,
Goaded by restless hunger, far and wide
Range all disordered thro' the town, to snatch
Such victual and such rest as chance may give
Within the captive halls that once were Troy--
Joyful to rid them of the frost and dew,
Wherein they couched upon the plain of old--
Joyful to sleep the gracious night all through,
Unsummoned of the watching sentinel.
Yet let them reverence well the city's gods,
The lords of Troy, tho' fallen, and her shrines;
So shall the spoilers not in turn be spoiled.
Yea, let no craving for forbidden gain
Bid conquerors yield before the darts of greed.
For we need yet, before the race be won,
Homewards, unharmed, to round the course once more.
For should the host wax wanton ere it come,
Then, tho' the sudden blow of fate be spared,
Yet in the sight of gods shall rise once more

The great wrong of the slain, to claim revenge.
Now, hearing from this woman's mouth of mine,
The tale and eke its warning, pray with me,
"Luck sway the scale, with no uncertain poise.
For my fair hopes are changed to fairer joys."

Chorus:

A gracious word thy woman's lips have told,
Worthy a wise man's utterance, O my queen;
Now with clear trust in thy convincing tale
I set me to salute the gods with song,
Who bring us bliss to counterpoise our pain.

Exit Clytemnestra.

Zeus, Lord of heaven! and welcome night
Of victory, that hast our might
With all the glories crowned!
On towers of Ilion, free no more,
Hast flung the mighty mesh of war,
And closely girt them round,
Till neither warrior may 'scape,
Nor stripling lightly overleap
The trammels as they close, and close,
Till with the grip of doom our foes
In slavery's coil are bound!

Zeus, Lord of hospitality,
In grateful awe I bend to thee--
Tis thou hast struck the blow!
At Alexander, long ago,
We marked thee bend thy vengeful bow,
But long and warily withhold
The eager shaft, which, uncontrolled
And loosed too soon or launched too high,
Had wandered bloodless through the sky.

Zeus, the high God!--whate'er be dim in doubt,
This can our thought track out--
The blow that fells the sinner is of God,
And as he wills, the rod

Of vengeance smiteth sore.One said of old,
"The gods list not to hold
A reckoning with him whose feet oppress
The grace of holiness--"
An impious word! for whensoe'er the sire
Breathed forth rebellious fire--
What time his household overflowed the measure
Of bliss and health and treasure--
His children's children read the reckoning plain,
At last, in tears and pain.
On me let weal that brings no woe be sent,

And therewithal, content!
Who spurns the shrine of Right, nor wealth nor power
Shall be to him a tower,
To guard him from the gulf: there lies his lot,
Where all things are forgot.
Lust drives him on--lust, desperate and wild,
Fate's sin-contriving child--
And cure is none; beyond concealment clear,
Kindles sin's baleful glare.
As an ill coin beneath the wearing touch
Betrays by stain and smutch
Its metal false--such is the sinful wight.
Before, on pinions light,
Fair Pleasure flits, and lures him childlike on,
While home and kin make moan
Beneath the grinding burden of his crime;
Till, in the end of time,
Cast down of heaven, he pours forth fruitless prayer
To powers that will not hear.

And such did Paris come
Unto Atrides' home,
And thence, with sin and shame his welcome to repay,
Ravished the wife away--
And she, unto her country and her kin
Leaving the clash of shields and spears and arming ships,
And bearing unto Troy destruction for a dower,
And overbold in sin,
Went fleetly thro' the gates, at midnight hour.
Oft from the prophets' lips
Moaned out the warning and the wail--Ah woe!
Woe for the home, the home! and for the chieftains, woe
Woe for the bride-bed, warm
Yet from the lovely limbs, the impress of the form
Of her who loved her lord, a while ago!
And woe! for him who stands
Shamed, silent, unreproachful, stretching hands
That find her not, and sees, yet will not see,
That she is far away!

And his sad fancy, yearning o'er the sea,
Shall summon and recall
Her wraith, once more to queen it in his hall.
And sad with many memories,
The fair cold beauty of each sculptured face--
And all to hatefulness is turned their grace,
Seen blankly by forlorn and hungering eyes!
And when the night is deep,
Come visions, sweet and sad, and bearing pain
Of hopings vain--
Void, void and vain, for scarce the sleeping sight
Has seen its old delight,
When thro' the grasps of love that bid it stay
It vanishes away
On silent wings that roam adown the ways of sleep.

Such are the sights, the sorrows fell,
About our hearth--and worse, whereof I may not tell.
But, all the wide town o'er,
Each home that sent its master far away
From Hellas' shore,
Feels the keen thrill of heart, the pang of loss, to-day.
For, truth to say,
The touch of bitter death is manifold!
Familiar was each face, and dear as life,
That went unto the war,
But thither, whence a warrior went of old,
Doth nought return--
Only a spear and sword, and ashes in an urn!
For Ares, lord of strife,
Who doth the swaying scales of battle hold,
War's money-changer, giving dust for gold,
Sends back, to hearts that held them dear,
Scant ash of warriors, wept with many a tear,
Light to the hand, but heavy to the soul;
Yea, fills the light urn full
With what survived the flame--
Death's dusty measure of a hero's frame!

"Alas!" one cries, "and yet alas again!
Our chief is gone, the hero of the spear,
And hath not left his peer!
Ah woe!" another moans--"my spouse is slain,
The death of honour, rolled in dust and blood,
Slain for a woman's sin, a false wife's shame!"
Such muttered words of bitter mood
Rise against those who went forth to reclaim;
Yea, jealous wrath creeps on against th' Atrides' name.

And others, far beneath the Ilian wall,
Sleep their last sleep--the goodly chiefs and tall,
Couched in the foeman's land, whereon they gave
Their breath, and lords of Troy, each in his Trojan grave.

Therefore for each and all the city's breast
Is heavy with a wrath supprest,
As deep and deadly as a curse more loud
Flung by the common crowd;
And, brooding deeply, doth my soul await
Tidings of coming fate,
Buried as yet in darkness' womb.
For not forgetful is the high gods' doom
Against the sons of carnage: all too long
Seems the unjust to prosper and be strong,
Till the dark Furies come,
And smite with stern reversal all his home,
Down into dim obstruction--he is gone,
And help and hope, among the lost, is none!

O'er him who vaunteth an exceeding fame,
Impends a woe condign;
The vengeful bolt upon his eyes doth flame,
Sped from the hand divine.
This bliss be mine, ungrudged of God, to feel--
To tread no city to the dust,
Nor see my own life thrust
Down to a slave's estate beneath another's heel!

Behold, throughout the city wide
Have the swift feet of Rumour hied,
Roused by the joyful flame:
But is the news they scatter, sooth?
Or haply do they give for truth
Some cheat which heaven doth frame?
A child were he and all unwise,
Who let his heart with joy be stirred,
To see the beacon-fires arise,
And then, beneath some thwarting word,
Sicken anon with hope deferred.
The edge of woman's insight still
Good news from true divideth ill;
Light rumours leap within the bound
That fences female credence round,
But, lightly born, as lightly dies
The tale that springs of her surmise.

Soon shall we know whereof the bale-fires tell,
The beacons, kindled with transmitted flame;
Whether, as well I deem, their tale is true.
Or whether like some dream delusive came
The welcome blaze but to befool our soul.
For lo! I see a herald from the shore
Draw hither, shadowed with the olive-wreath--
And thirsty dust, twin-brother of the clay,
Speaks plain of travel far and truthful news--
No dumb surmise, nor tongue of flame in smoke,
Fitfully kindled from the mountain pyre;
But plainlier shall his voice say, "All is well,"
Or--but away, forebodings adverse, now,

And on fair promise fair fulfilment come!
And whoso for the state prays otherwise,
Himself reap harvest of his ill desire!

Enter Herald:

O land of Argos, fatherland of mine!

To thee at last, beneath the tenth year's sun,
My feet return; the bark of my emprise,
Tho' one by one hope's anchors broke away,
Held by the last, and now rides safely here.
Long, long my soul despaired to win, in death,
Its longed-for rest within our Argive land:
And now all hail, O earth, and hail to thee,
New-risen sun! and hail our country's God,
High-ruling Zeus, and thou, the Pythian lord,
Whose arrows smote us once--smite thou no more!
Was not thy wrath wreaked full upon our heads,
O king Apollo, by Scamander's side?
Turn thou, be turned, be saviour, healer, now!
And hail, all gods who rule the street and mart
And Hermes hail! my patron and my pride,
Herald of heaven, and lord of heralds here!
And Heroes, ye who sped us on our way--
To one and all I cry, "Receive again
With grace such Argives as the spear has spared."

Ah, home of royalty, beloved halls,
And solemn shrines, and gods that front the morn!
Benign as erst, with sun-flushed aspect greet
The king returning after many days.
For as from night flash out the beams of day,
So out of darkness dawns a light, a king,
On you, on Argos--Agamemnon comes.
Then hail and greet him well! such meed befits
Him whose right hand hewed down the towers of Troy
With the great axe of Zeus who righteth wrong--
And smote the plain, smote down to nothingness
Each altar, every shrine; and far and wide
Dies from the whole land's face its offspring fair.

Such mighty yoke of fate he set on Troy--
Our lord and monarch, Atreus' elder son,
And comes at last with blissful honour home;
Highest of all who walk on earth to-day--
Not Paris nor the city's self that paid

22

Sin's price with him, can boast, "Whate'er befal,
The guerdon we have won outweighs it all."
But at Fate's judgment-seat the robber stands
Condemned of rapine, and his prey is torn
Forth from his hands, and by his deed is reaped
A bloody harvest of his home and land
Gone down to death, and for his guilt and lust
His father's race pays double in the dust.

Chorus:

Hail, herald of the Greeks, new-come from war.

Herald:

All hail! not death itself can fright me now.

Chorus:

Was thine heart wrung with longing for thy land?

Herald:

So that this joy doth brim mine eyes with tears.

Chorus:

On you too then this sweet distress did fall--

Herald:

How say'st thou? make me master of thy word.

Chorus:

You longed for us who pined for you again.

Herald:

Craved the land us who craved it, love for love?

Chorus:

Yea till my brooding heart moaned out with pain.

Herald:

Whence thy despair, that mars the army's joy?

Chorus:

"Sole cure of wrong is silence," saith the saw.

Herald:

Thy kings afar, couldst thou fear other men?

Chorus:

Death had been sweet, as thou didst say but now.

Herald:

'Tis true; Fate smiles at last. Throughout our toil,
These many years, some chances issued fair,
And some, I wot, were chequered with a curse.
But who, on earth, hath won the bliss of heaven,
Thro' time's whole tenor an unbroken weal?
I could a tale unfold of toiling oars,
Ill rest, scant landings on a shore rock-strewn,
All pains, all sorrows, for our daily doom.
And worse and hatefuller our woes on land;
For where we couched, close by the foeman's wall,
The river-plain was ever dank with dews,
Dropped from the sky, exuded from the earth,
A curse that clung unto our sodden garb,
And hair as horrent as a wild beast's fell.
Why tell the woes of winter, when the birds

Lay stark and stiff, so stern was Ida's snow?
Or summer's scorch, what time the stirless wave
Sank to its sleep beneath the noon-day sun?
Why mourn old woes? their pain has passed away;
And passed away, from those who fell, all care,
For evermore, to rise and live again.

Why sum the count of death, and render thanks
For life by moaning over fate malign?
Farewell, a long farewell to all our woes!
To us, the remnant of the host of Greece,
Comes weal beyond all counterpoise of woe;
Thus boast we rightfully to yonder sun,
Like him far-fleeted over sea and land.
"The Argive host prevailed to conquer Troy,
And in the temples of the gods of Greece
Hung up these spoils, a shining sign to Time."
Let those who learn this legend bless aright
The city and its chieftains, and repay
The meed of gratitude to Zeus who willed
And wrought the deed. So stands the tale fulfilled.

Chorus:

Thy words o'erbear my doubt: for news of good,
The ear of age hath ever youth enow:
But those within and Clytemnestra's self
Would fain hear all; glad thou their ears and mine.

Re-enter 'Clytemnestra:

Last night, when first the fiery courier came,
In sign that Troy is ta'en and razed to earth,
So wild a cry of joy my lips gave out,
That I was chidden--"Hath the beacon watch
Made sure unto thy soul the sack of Troy?
A very woman thou, whose heart leaps light
At wandering rumours!"--and with words like these
They showed me how I strayed, misled of hope.

Yet on each shrine I set the sacrifice,
And, in the strain they held for feminine,
Went heralds thro' the city, to and fro,
With voice of loud proclaim, announcing joy;
And in each fane they lit and quenched with wine
The spicy perfumes fading in the flame.   .
All is fulfilled: I spare your longer tale--
The king himself anon shall tell me all.

Remains to think what honour best may greet
My lord, the majesty of Argos, home.
What day beams fairer on a woman's eyes
Than this, whereon she flings the portal wide,
To hail her lord, heaven-shielded, home from war?
This to my husband, that he tarry not,
But turn the city's longing into joy!
Yea let him come, and coming may he find
A wife no other than he left her, true
And faithful as a watch-dog to his home,
His foemen's foe, in all her duties leal,
Trusty to keep for ten long years unmarred
The store whereon he set his master-seal.
Be steel deep-dyed, before ye look to see
Ill joy, ill fame, from other wight, in me!

Herald:

'Tis fairly said: thus speaks a noble dame,
Nor speaks amiss, when truth informs the boast.

Exit Clytemnestra.

Chorus:

So has she spoken--be it yours to learn
By clear interpreters her specious word.
Turn to me, herald--tell me if anon
The second well-loved lord of Argos comes?
Hath Menelaus safely sped with you?

Herald:

Alas--brief boon unto my friends it were,
To flatter them, for truth, with falsehoods fair!

Chorus:

Speak joy, if truth be joy, but truth, at worst--
loo plainly, truth and joy are here divorced.

Herald:

The hero and his bark were rapt away
Far from the Grecian fleet? 'tis truth I say.

Chorus:

Whether in all men's sight from Ilion borne,
Or from the fleet by stress of weather torn?

Herald:

Full on the mark thy shaft of speech doth light,
And one short word hath told long woes aright.

Chorus:

But say, what now of him each comrade saith?
What their forebodings, of his life or death?

Herald:

Ask me no more: the truth is known to none,
Save the earth-fostering, all-surveying Sun,
Chorus:

Say, by what doom the fleet of Greece was driven?
How rose, how sank the storm, the wrath of heaven?

Herald:

Nay, ill it were to mar with sorrow's tale
The day of blissful news. The gods demand
Thanksgiving sundered from solicitude.
If one as herald came with rueful face
To say, "The curse has fallen, and the host
Gone down to death; and one wide wound has reached
The city's heart, and out of many homes
Many are cast and consecrate to death,
Beneath the double scourge, that Ares loves,
The bloody pair, the fire and sword of doom"--
If such sore burden weighed upon my tongue,
'Twere fit to speak such words as gladden fiends.
But--coming as he comes who bringeth news
Of safe return from toil, and issues fair,
To men rejoicing in a weal restored--
Dare I to dash good words with ill, and say
How the gods' anger smote the Greeks in storm?
For fire and sea, that erst held bitter feud,
Now swore conspiracy and pledged their faith,
Wasting the Argives worn with toil and war.
Night and great horror of the rising wave
Came o'er us, and the blasts that blow from Thrace
Clashed ship with ship, and some with plunging prow
Thro' scudding drifts of spray and raving storm
Vanished, as strays by some ill shepherd driven.
And when at length the sun rose bright, we saw
Th' Aegaean sea-field flecked with flowers of death,
Corpses of Grecian men and shattered hulls.
For us indeed, some god, as well I deem,
No human power, laid hand upon our helm,
Snatched us or prayed us from the powers of air,
And brought our bark thro' all, unharmed in hull:
And saving Fortune sat and steered us fair,
So that no surge should gulf us deep in brine,
Nor grind our keel upon a rocky shore.

So 'scaped we death that lurks beneath the sea,
But, under day's white light, mistrustful all
Of fortune's smile, we sat and brooded deep,
Shepherds forlorn of thoughts that wandered wild,
O'er this new woe; for smitten was our host,
And lost as ashes scattered from the pyre.
Of whom if any draw his life-breath yet,
Be well assured, he deems of us as dead,
As we of him no other fate forebode.
But heaven save all! If Menelaus live,
He will not tarry, but will surely come:
Therefore if anywhere the high sun's ray
Descries him upon earth, preserved by Zeus,
Who wills not yet to wipe his race away,
Hope still there is that homeward he may wend.
Enough--thou hast the truth unto the end.

Chorus:

Say, from whose lips the presage fell?
Who read the future all too well,
And named her, in her natal hour,
Helen, the bride with war for dower?
Twas one of the Invisible,
Guiding his tongue with prescient power.
On fleet, and host, and citadel,
War, sprung from her, and death did lour,
When from the bride-bed's fine-spun veil
She to the Zephyr spread her sail.

Strong blew the breeze--the surge closed o'er
The cloven track of keel and oar,
But while she fled, there drove along,
Fast in her wake, a mighty throng--
Athirst for blood, athirst for war,
Forward in fell pursuit they sprung,
Then leapt on Simois' bank ashore,
The leafy coppices among--
No rangers, they, of wood and field,

But huntsmen of the sword and shield.

Heaven's jealousy, that works its will,
Sped thus on Troy its destined ill,
Well named, at once, the Bride and Bane;
And loud rang out the bridal strain;
But they to whom that song befel
Did turn anon to tears again;
Zeus tarries, but avenges still
The husband's wrong, the household's stain!
He, the hearth's lord, brooks not to see
Its outraged hospitality.

Even now, and in far other tone,
Troy chants her dirge of mighty moan,
"Woe upon Paris, woe and hate!
Who wooed his country's doom for mate"--
This is the burthen of the groan,
Wherewith she wails disconsolate
The blood, so many of her own
Have poured in vain, to fend her fate;
Troy! thou hast fed and freed to roam
A lion-cub within thy home!

A suckling creature, newly ta'en
From mother's teat, still fully fain
Of nursing care; and oft caressed,
Within the arms, upon the breast,
Even as an infant, has it lain;
Or fawns and licks, by hunger pressed,
The hand that will assuage its pain;
In life's young dawn, a well-loved guest,
A fondling for the children's play,
A joy unto the old and gray.

But waxing time and growth betrays
The blood-thirst of the lion-race,
And, for the house's fostering care,
Unbidden all, it revels there,

And bloody recompense repays--
Rent flesh of tine, its talons tare:
A mighty beast, that slays and slays,
And mars with blood the household fair,
A God-sent pest invincible,
A minister of fate and hell.

Even so to Ilion's city came by stealth
A spirit as of windless seas and skies,
A gentle phantom-form of joy and wealth,
With love's soft arrows speeding from its eyes--
Love's rose, whose thorn doth pierce the soul in subtle wise.

Ah, well-a-day! the bitter bridal-bed,
When the fair mischief lay by Paris' side!
What curse on palace and on people sped
With her, the Fury sent on Priam's pride,
By angered Zeus! what tears of many a widowed bride!

Long, long ago to mortals this was told,
How sweet security and blissful state
Have curses for their children--so men hold--
And for the man of all-too prosperous fate
Springs from a bitter seed some woe insatiate.

Alone, alone, I deem far otherwise;
Not bliss nor wealth it is, but impious deed,
From which that after-growth of ill doth rise!
Woe springs from wrong, the plant is like the seed--
While Right, in honour's house, doth its own likeness breed.

Some past impiety, some gray old crime,
Breeds the young curse, that wantons in our ill,
Early or late, when haps th' appointed time--
And out of light brings power of darkness still,
A master-fiend, a foe, unseen, invincible;

A pride accursed, that broods upon the race
And home in which dark Atè holds her sway--

Sin's child and Woe's, that wears its parents' face;
While Right in smoky cribs shines clear as day,
And decks with weal his life, who walks the righteous way.

From gilded halls, that hands polluted raise,
Right turns away with proud averted eyes,
And of the wealth, men stamp amiss with praise,
Heedless, to poorer, holier temples hies,
And to Fate's goal guides all, in its appointed wise.

Hail to thee, chief of Atreus' race,
Returning proud from Troy subdued!
How shall I greet thy conquering face,
How nor a fulsome praise obtrude,
Nor stint the meed of gratitude?
For mortal men who fall to ill
Take little heed of open truth,
But seek unto its semblance still:
The show of weeping and of ruth
To the forlorn will all men pay,
But, of the grief their eyes display,
Nought to the heart doth pierce its way.
And, with the joyous, they beguile
Their lips unto a feigned smile,
And force a joy, unfelt the while;
But he who as a shepherd wise
Doth know his flock, can ne'er misread
Truth in the falsehood of his eyes,
Who veils beneath a kindly guise
A lukewarm love in deed.
And thou, our leader--when of yore
Thou badest Greece go forth to war
For Helen's sake--I dare avow
That then I held thee not as now;
That to my vision thou didst seem
Dyed in the hues of disesteem.
I held thee for a pilot ill,
And reckless, of thy proper will,
Endowing others doomed to die

With vain and forced audacity!
Now from my heart, ungrudgingly,
To those that wrought, this word be said--
"Well fall the labour ye have sped--"
Let time and search, O king, declare
What men within thy city's bound
Were loyal to the kingdom's care,
And who were faithless found.

Enter Agamemnon in a chariot, accompanied by Cassandra.
He speaks without descending.

Agamemnon:

First, as is meet, a king's All-hail be said
To Argos, and the gods that guard the land--
Gods who with me availed to speed us home,
With me availed to wring from Priam's town
The due of justice. In the court of heaven
The gods in conclave sat and judged the cause,
Not from a pleader's tongue, and at the close,
Unanimous into the urn of doom
This sentence gave, "On Ilion and her men,
Death:" and where hope drew nigh to pardon's urn
No hand there was to cast a vote therein.
And still the smoke of fallen Ilion
Rises in sight of all men, and the flame
Of Atè's hecatomb is living yet,
And where the towers in dusty ashes sink,
Rise the rich fumes of pomp and wealth consumed.
For this must all men pay unto the gods
The meed of mindful hearts and gratitude:
For by our hands the meshes of revenge
Closed on the prey, and for one woman's sake
Troy trodden by the Argive monster lies--
The foal, the shielded band that leapt the wall,
What time with autumn sank the Pleiades.
Yea, o'er the fencing wall a lion sprang
Ravening, and lapped his fill of blood of kings.

Such prelude spoken to the gods in full,
To you I turn, and to the hidden thing
Whereof ye spake but now: and in that thought
I am as you, and what ye say, say I.
For few are they who have such inborn grace,
As to look up with love, and envy not,
When stands another on the height of weal.
Deep in his heart, whom jealousy hath seized,
Her poison lurking doth enhance his load;
For now beneath his proper woes he chafes,
And sighs withal to see another's weal.

Agamemnon:

I speak not idly, but from knowledge sure--
There be who vaunt an utter loyalty,
That is but as the ghost of friendship dead,
A shadow in a glass, of faith gone by.
One only--he who went reluctant forth
Across the seas with me--Odysseus--he
Was loyal unto me with strength and will,
A trusty trace-horse bound unto my car.
Thus--be he yet beneath the light of day,
Or dead, as well I fear--I speak his praise.

Lastly, whate'er be due to men or gods,
With joint debate, in public council held,
We will decide, and warily contrive
That all which now is well may so abide:
For that which haply needs the healer's art,
That will we medicine, discerning well
If cautery or knife befit the time.

Now, to my palace and the shrines of home,
I will pass in, and greet you first and fair,
Ye gods, who bade me forth, and home again--
And long may Victory tarry in my train!

Enter Clytemnestra, followed by maidens bearing purple robes.

Clytemnestra:

Old men of Argos, lieges of our realm,
Shame shall not bid me shrink lest ye should see
The love I bear my lord. Such blushing fear
Dies at the last from hearts of human kind.
From mine own soul and from no alien lips,
I know and will reveal the life I bore,
Reluctant, through the lingering livelong years,
The while my lord beleaguered Ilion's wall.

First, that a wife sat sundered from her lord,
In widowed solitude, was utter woe--
And woe, to hear how rumour's many tongues
All boded evil--woe, when he who came
And he who followed spake of ill on ill,
Keening "Lost, lost, all lost!" thro' hail and bower.
Had this my husband met so many wounds,
As by a thousand channels rumour told,
No network e'er was full of holes as he.
Had he been slain, as oft as tidings came
That he was dead, he well might boast him now
A second Geryon of triple frame,
With triple robe of earth above him laid--
For that below, no matter--triply dead,
Dead by one death for every form he bore.
And thus distraught by news of wrath and woe,
Oft for self-slaughter had I slung the noose,
But others wrenched it from my neck away.
Hence haps it that Orestes, thine and mine,
The pledge and symbol of our wedded troth,
Stands not beside us now, as he should stand.
Nor marvel thou at this: he dwells with one
Who guards him loyally; 'tis Phocis' king,
Strophius, who warned me erst, "Bethink thee, queen,
What woes of doubtful issue well may fall!
Thy lord in daily jeopardy at Troy,

While here a populace uncurbed may cry
"Down with the council, down!" bethink thee too,
Tis the world's way to set a harder heel
On fallen power."
For thy child's absence then
Such mine excuse, no wily afterthought.
For me, long since the gushing fount of tears
Is wept away; no drop is left to shed.
Dim are the eyes that ever watched till dawn,
Weeping, the bale-fires, piled for thy return,
Night after night unkindled. If I slept,
Each sound--the tiny humming of a gnat,
Roused me again, again, from fitful dreams
Wherein I felt thee smitten, saw thee slain,
Thrice for each moment of mine hour of sleep.

All this I bore, and now, released from woe,
I hail my lord as watch-dog of a fold,
As saving stay-rope of a storm-tossed ship,
As column stout that holds the roof aloft,
As only child unto a sire bereaved,
As land beheld, past hope, by crews forlorn,
As sunshine fair when tempest's wrath is past,
As gushing spring to thirsty wayfarer.
So sweet it is to 'scape the press of pain.
With such salute I bid my husband hail!
Nor heaven be wroth therewith! for long and hard
I bore that ire of old.
Sweet lord, step forth,
Step from thy car, I pray--nay, not on earth
Plant the proud foot, O king, that trod down Troy!
Women! why tarry ye, whose task it is
To spread your monarch's path with tapestry?
Swift, swift, with purple strew his passage fair,
That justice lead him to a home, at last,
He scarcely looked to see.
For what remains,
Zeal unsubdued by sleep shall nerve my hand
To work as right and as the gods command.

Agamemnon:

Daughter of Leda, watcher o'er my home,
Thy greeting well befits mine absence long,
For late and hardly has it reached its end.
Know, that the praise which honour bids us crave,
Must come from others' lips, not from our own:
See too that not in fashion feminine
Thou make a warrior's pathway delicate;
Not unto me, as to some Eastern lord,
Bowing thyself to earth, make homage loud.
Strew not this purple that shall make each step
An arrogance; such pomp beseems the gods,
Not me. A mortal man to set his foot
On these rich dyes? I hold such pride in fear,
And bid thee honour me as man, not god.

Fear not--such footcloths and all gauds apart,
Loud from the trump of Fame my name is blown;
Best gift of heaven it is, in glory's hour,
To think thereon with soberness: and thou?
Bethink thee of the adage, "Call none blest
Till peaceful death have crowned a life of weal."
Tis said: I fain would fare unvexed by fear.

Clytemnestra:

Nay, but unsay it--thwart not thou my will!

Agamemnon:

Know, I have said, and will not mar my word.

Clytemnestra:

Was it fear made this meekness to the gods?

Agamemnon:

If cause be cause, 'tis mine for this resolve.

Clytemnestra:

What, think'st thou, in thy place had Priam done?

Agamemnon:

He surely would have walked on broidered robes.

Clytemnestra:

Then fear not thou the voice of human blame.

Agamemnon:

Yet mighty is the murmur of a crowd.

Clytemnestra:

Shrink not from envy, appanage of bliss.

Agamemnon:

War is not woman's part, nor war of words.

Clytemnestra:

Yet happy victors well may yield therein.

Agamemnon:

Dost crave for triumph in this petty strife?

Clytemnestra:

Yield; of thy grace permit me to prevail!

Agamemnon:

Then, if thou wilt, let some one stoop to loose
Swiftly these sandals, slaves beneath my foot:
And stepping thus upon the sea's rich dye,
I pray, "Let none among the gods look down
With jealous eye on me"--reluctant all,
To trample thus and mar a thing of price,
Wasting the wealth of garments silver-worth.
Enough hereof: and, for the stranger maid,
Lead her within, but gently: God on high
Looks graciously on him whom triumph's hour
Has made not pitiless. None willingly
Wear the slave's yoke--and she, the prize and flower
Of all we won, comes hither in my train,
Gift of the army to its chief and lord.
--Now, since in this my will bows down to thine,
I will pass in on purples to my home.

Clytemnestra:

A Sea there is--and who shall stay its springs?
And deep within its breast, a mighty store,
Precious as silver, of the purple dye,
Whereby the dipped robe doth its tint renew.
Enough of such, O king, within thy halls
There lies, a store that cannot fail; but I--
I would have gladly vowed unto the gods
Cost of a thousand garments trodden thus,
(Had once the oracle such gift required)
Contriving ransom for thy life preserved.
For while the stock is firm the foliage climbs,
Spreading a shade what time the dog-star glows;
And thou, returning to thine hearth and home,
Art as a genial warmth in winter hours,
Or as a coolness, when the lord of heaven
Mellows the juice within the bitter grape.
Such boons and more doth bring into a home
The present footstep of its proper lord.

Zeus, Zeus, Fulfilment's lord! my vows fulfil,
And whatsoe'er it be, work forth thy will!

Exeunt all but Cassandra and the Chorus.

Chorus:

Wherefore for ever on the wings of fear
Hovers a vision drear
Before my boding heart? a strain,
Unbidden and unwelcome, thrills mine ear,
Oracular of pain.
Not as of old upon my bosom's throne
Sits Confidence, to spurn
Such fears, like dreams we know not to discern.
Old, old and gray long since the time has grown,
Which saw the linked cables moor
The fleet, when erst it came to Ilion's sandy shore;
And now mine eyes and not another's see
Their safe return.

Yet none the less in me
The inner spirit sings a boding song,
Self-prompted, sings the Furies' strain--
And seeks, and seeks in vain,
To hope and to be strong!

Ah! to some end of Fate, unseen, unguessed,
Are these wild throbbings of my heart and breast?
Yea, of some doom they tell?
Each pulse, a knell.
Lief, lief I were, that all
To unfulfilment's hidden realm might fall.

Too far, too far our mortal spirits strive,
Grasping at utter weal, unsatisfied--
Till the fell curse, that dwelleth hard beside,
Thrust down the sundering wall. Too fair they blow,
The gales that waft our bark on Fortune's tide!

Swiftly we sail, the sooner all to drive
Upon the hidden rock, the reef of woe.

Then if the hand of caution warily
Sling forth into the sea
Part of the freight, lest all should sink below,
From the deep death it saves the bark: even so,
Doom-laden though it be, once more may rise
His household, who is timely wise.

How oft the famine-stricken field
Is saved by God's large gift, the new year's yield!
But blood of man once spilled,
Once at his feet shed forth, and darkening the plain,--
Nor chant nor charm can call it back again.

So Zeus hath willed:
Else had he spared the leech Asclepius, skilled
To bring man from the dead: the hand divine
Did smite himself with death--a warning and a sign.

Ah me! if Fate, ordained of old,
Held not the will of gods constrained, controlled,
Helpless to us ward, and apart--
Swifter than speech my heart
Had poured its presage out!
Now, fretting, chafing in the dark of doubt,
Tis hopeless to unfold
Truth, from fear's tangled skein; and, yearning to proclaim
Its thought, my soul is prophecy and flame.

Re-enter 'Clytemnestra:

Get thee within thou too, Cassandra, go!
For Zeus to thee in gracious mercy grants
To share the sprinklings of the lustral bowl,
Beside the altar of his guardianship,
Slave among many slaves. What, haughty still?
Step from the car; Alcmena's son, 'tis said,

Was sold perforce and bore the yoke of old.
Ay, hard it is, but, if such fate befall,
'Tis a fair chance to serve within a home
Of ancient wealth and power. An upstart lord,
To whom wealth's harvest came beyond his hope,
Is as a lion to his slaves, in all
Exceeding fierce, immoderate in sway.
Pass in: thou hearest what our ways will be.

Chorus:

Clear unto thee, O maid, is her command,
But thou--within the toils of Fate thou art--
If such thy will, I urge thee to obey;
Yet I misdoubt thou dost nor hear nor heed.

Clytemnestra:

I wot--unless like swallows she doth use
Some strange barbarian tongue from oversea--
My words must speak persuasion to her soul.

Chorus:

Obey: there is no gentler way than this.
Step from the car's high seat and follow her.

Clytemnestra:

Truce to this bootless waiting here without!
I will not stay: beside the central shrine
The victims stand, prepared for knife and fire--
Offerings from hearts beyond all hope made glad.
Thou--if thou reckest aught of my command,
'Twere well done soon: but if thy sense be shut
From these my words, let thy barbarian hand
Fulfil by gesture the default of speech.

Chorus:

No native is she, thus to read thy words
Unaided: like some wild thing of the wood,
New-trapped, behold! she shrinks and glares on thee.

Clytemnestra:

'Tis madness and the rule of mind distraught,
Since she beheld her city sink in fire,
And hither comes, nor brooks the bit, until
In foam and blood her wrath be champed away.
See ye to her; unqueenly 'tis for me,
Unheeded thus to cast away my words.

Exit Clytemnestra.

Chorus:

But with me pity sits in anger's place.
Poor maiden, come thou from the car; no way
There is but this--take up thy servitude.

Cassandra:

Woe, woe, alas! Earth, Mother Earth! and thou
Apollo, Apollo!

Chorus:

Peace! shriek not to the bright prophetic god,
Who will not brook the suppliance of woe.

Cassandra:

Woe, woe, alas! Earth, Mother Earth! and thou
Apollo, Apollo!

Chorus:

Hark, with wild curse she calls anew on him,
Who stands far off and loathes the voice of wail.

Cassandra:

Apollo, Apollo!
God of all ways, but only Death's to me,
Once and again, O thou, Destroyer named,
Thou hast destroyed me, thou, my love of old!

Chorus:

She grows presageful of her woes to come,
Slave tho' she be, instinct with prophecy.

Cassandra:

Apollo, Apollo!
God of all ways, but only Death's to me,
O thou Apollo, thou Destroyer named!
What way hast led me, to what evil home?

Chorus:

Know'st thou it not? The home of Atreus' race:
Take these my words for sooth and ask no more.

Cassandra:

Home cursed of God! Bear witness unto me,
Ye visioned woes within--
The blood-stained hands of them that smite their kin--
The strangling noose, and, spattered o'er
With human blood, the reeking floor!

Chorus:

How like a sleuth-hound questing on the track,
Keen-scented unto blood and death she hies!

Cassandra:

Ah! can the ghostly guidance fail,
Whereby my prophet-soul is onwards led?
Look! for their flesh the spectre-children wail,
Their sodden limbs on which their father fed!

Chorus:

Long since we knew of thy prophetic fame,--
But for those deeds we seek no prophet's tongue.

Cassandra:

God! 'tis another crime--
Worse than the storied woe of olden time,
Curelessabhorred, that one is plotting here--
A shaming death, for those that should be dear!
Alas! and far away, in foreign land,
He that should help doth stand!

Chorus:

I knew th' old tales, the city rings withal--
But now thy speech is dark, beyond my ken.

Cassandra:

O wretch, O purpose fell!
Thou for thy wedded lord
The cleansing wave hast poured--
A treacherous welcome!
How the sequel tell?
Too soon 'twill come, too soon, for now, even now,
She smites him, blow on blow!

Chorus:

Riddles beyond my rede--I peer in vain
Thro' the dim films that screen the prophecy.

Cassandra:

God! a new sight! a net, a snare of hell,
Set by her hand--herself a snare more fell!
A wedded wife, she slays her lord,
Helped by another hand!
Ye powers, whose hate
Of Atreus' home no blood can satiate,
Raise the wild cry above the sacrifice abhorred!

Chorus:

Why biddest thou some fiend, I know not whom,
Shriek o'er the house? Thine is no cheering word.
Back to my heart in frozen fear I feel
My waning life-blood run--
The blood that round the wounding steel
Ebbs slow, as sinks life's parting sun--
Swift, swift and sure, some woe comes pressing on!

Cassandra:

Away, away--keep him away--
The monarch of the herd, the pasture's pride,
Far from his mate! In treach'rous wrath,
Muffling his swarthy horns, with secret scathe
She gores his fenceless side!
Hark! in the brimming bath,
The heavy plash--the dying cry--
Hark--in the laver--hark, he falls by treachery!

Chorus:

I read amiss dark sayings such as thine,
Yet something warns me that they tell of ill.
O dark prophetic speech,

Ill tidings dost thou teach
Ever, to mortals here below!
Ever some tale of awe and woe
Thro' all thy windings manifold
Do we unriddle and unfold!

Cassandra:

Ah well-a-day! the cup of agony,
Whereof I chant, foams with a draught for me.
Ah lord, ah leader, thou hast led me here--
Was't but to die with thee whose doom is near?

Chorus:

Distraught thou art, divinely stirred,
And wailest for thyself a tuneless lay,
As piteous as the ceaseless tale
Wherewith the brown melodious bird
Doth ever Itys! Itys! wail,
Deep-bowered in sorrow, all its little life-time's day!

Cassandra:

Ah for thy fate, O shrill-voiced nightingale!
Some solace for thy woes did Heaven afford,
Clothed thee with soft brown plumes, and life apart from wail?
But for my death is edged the double-biting sword!

Chorus:

What pangs are these, what fruitless pain,
Sent on thee from on high?
Thou chantest terror's frantic strain,
Yet in shrill measured melody.
How thus unerring canst thou sweep along
The prophet's path of boding song?

Cassandra:

Woe, Paris, woe on thee! thy bridal joy
Was death and fire upon thy race and Troy!
And woe for thee, Scamander's flood!
Beside thy banks, O river fair,
I grew in tender nursing care
From childhood unto maidenhood!
Now not by thine, but by Cocytus' stream
And Acheron's banks shall ring my boding scream.

Chorus:

Too plain is all, too plain!
A child might read aright thy fateful strain.
Deep in my heart their piercing fang
Terror and sorrow set, the while I heard
That piteous, low, tender word,
Yet to mine ear and heart a crushing pang.

Cassandra:
Woe for my city, woe for Ilion's fall!
Father, how oft with sanguine stain
Streamed on thine altar-stone the blood of cattle, slain
That heaven might guard our wall!
But all was shed in vain.
Low lie the shattered towers whereas they fell,
And I--ah burning heart!--shall soon lie low as well.

Chorus:

Of sorrow is thy song, of sorrow still!
Alas, what power of ill
Sits heavy on thy heart and bids thee tell
In tears of perfect moan thy deadly tale?
Some woe--I know not what--must close thy piteous wail.

Cassandra:

List! for no more the presage of my soul,

Bride-like, shall peer from its secluding veil;
But as the morning wind blows clear the east,
More bright shall blow the wind of prophecy,
And as against the low bright line of dawn
Heaves high and higher yet the rolling wave,
So in the clearing skies of prescience
Dawns on my soul a further, deadlier woe,
And I will speak, but in dark speech no more.
Bear witness, ye, and follow at my side--
I scent the trail of blood, shed long ago.
Within this house a choir abidingly
Chants in harsh unison the chant of ill;
Yea, and they drink, for more enhardened joy,
Man's blood for wine, and revel in the halls,
Departing never, Furies of the home.
They sit within, they chant the primal curse,
Each spitting hatred on that crime of old,
The brother's couch, the love incestuous
That brought forth hatred to the ravisher.
Say, is my speech or wild and erring now,
Or doth its arrow cleave the mark indeed?
They called me once, "The prophetess of lies,
The wandering hag, the pest of every door--"
Attest ye now, She knows in very sooth
"The house's curse, the storied infamy."

Chorus:

Yet how should oath--how loyally soe'er
I swear it--aught avail thee? In good sooth,

Agamemnon:

My wonder meets thy claim: I stand amazed
That thou, a maiden born beyond the seas,
Dost as a native know and tell aright
Tales of a city of an alien tongue.

Cassandra:

That is my power--a boon Apollo gave.

Chorus:

God though he were, yearning for mortal maid?

Cassandra:

Ay! what seemed shame of old is shame no more.

Chorus:

Such finer sense suits not with slavery.

Cassandra:

He strove to win me, panting for my love.

Chorus:

Came ye by compact unto bridal joys?

Cassandra:

Nay--for I plighted troth, then foiled the god.

Chorus:

Wert thou already dowered with prescience?

Cassandra:

Yea--prophetess to Troy of all her doom.

Chorus:

How left thee then Apollo's wrath unscathed?

Cassandra:

I, false to him, seemed prophet false to all.

Chorus:

Not so--to us at least thy words seem sooth.

Cassandra:

Woe for me, woe! Again the agony--
Dread pain that sees the future all too well
With ghastly preludes whirls and racks my soul.
Behold ye--yonder on the palace roof
The spectre-children sitting--look, such things
As dreams are made on, phantoms as of babes,
Horrible shadows, that a kinsman's hand
Hath marked with murder, and their arms are full--
A rueful burden--see, they hold them up,
The entrails upon which their father fed!

For this, for this, I say there plots revenge
A coward lion, couching in the lair--
Guarding the gate against my master's foot--
My master--mine--I bear the slave's yoke now,
And he, the lord of ships, who trod down Troy,
Knows not the fawning treachery of tongue
Of this thing false and dog-like--how her speech
Glozes and sleeks her purpose, till she win
By ill fate's favour the desired chance,
Moving like Atè to a secret end.
O aweless soul! the woman slays her lord--
Woman? what loathsome monster of the earth
Were fit comparison? The double snake--
Or Scylla, where she dwells, the seaman's bane,
Girt round about with rocks? some hag of hell,
Raving a truceless curse upon her kin?
Hark--even now she cries exultingly
The vengeful cry that tells of battle turned--

How fain, forsooth, to greet her chief restored!
Nay then, believe me not: what skills belief
Or disbelief? Fate works its will--and thou
Wilt see and say in ruth, "Her tale was true."

Chorus:

Ah--'tis Thyestes' feast on kindred flesh--
I guess her meaning and with horror thrill,
Hearing no shadow'd hint of th' o'er-true tale,
But its full hatefulness: yet, for the rest,
Far from the track I roam, and know no more.

Cassandra:

'Tis Agamemnon's doom thou shalt behold.

Chorus:

Peace, hapless woman, to thy boding words!

Cassandra:

Far from my speech stands he who sains and saves.

Chorus:

Ay--were such doom at hand--which God forbid!

Cassandra:

Thou prayest idly--these move swift to slay.

Chorus:

What man prepares a deed of such despite?

Cassandra:

Fool! thus to read amiss mine oracles.

Chorus:

Deviser and device are dark to me.

Cassandra:

Dark! all too well I speak the Grecian tongue.

Chorus:

Ay--but in thine, as in Apollo's strains,
Familiar is the tongue, but dark the thought.

Cassandra:

Ah ah the fire! it waxes, nears me now--
Woe, woe for me, Apollo of the dawn!

Lo, how the woman-thing, the lioness
Couched with the wolf--her noble mate afar--
Will slay me, slave forlorn! Yea, like some witch
She drugs the cup of wrath, that slays her lord
With double death--his recompense for me!
Ay, 'tis for me, the prey he bore from Troy,
That she hath sworn his death, and edged the steel!
Ye wands, ye wreaths that cling around my neck,
Ye showed me prophetess yet scorned of all--
I stamp you into death, or e'er I die--
Down, to destruction!
Thus I stand revenged--
Go, crown some other with a prophet's woe.
Look! it is he, it is Apollo's self
Rending from me the prophet-robe he gave
God! while I wore it yet, thou saw'st me mocked
There at my home by each malicious mouth--
To all and each, an undivided scorn.
The name alike and fate of witch and cheat--

Woe, poverty, and famine--all I bore;
And at this last the god hath brought me here
Into death's toils, and what his love had made
His hate unmakes me now: and I shall stand
Not now before the altar of my home,
But me a slaughter-house and block of blood
Shall see hewn down, a reeking sacrifice.
Yet shall the gods have heed of me who die,
For by their will shall one requite my doom.
He, to avenge his father's blood outpoured,
Shall smite and slay with matricidal hand.
Ay, he shall come--tho' far away he roam,
A banished wanderer in a stranger's land--
To crown his kindred's edifice of ill,
Called home to vengeance by his father's fall:
Thus have the high gods sworn, and shall fulfil.

And now why mourn I, tarrying on earth,
Since first mine Ilion has found its fate
And I beheld, and those who won the wall
Pass to such issue as the gods ordain?
I too will pass and like them dare to die!

Turns and looks upon the palace door.

Portal of Hades, thus I bid thee hail!
Grant me one boon--a swift and mortal stroke,
That all unwrung by pain, with ebbing blood
Shed forth in quiet death, I close mine eyes.

Chorus:

Maid of mysterious woes, mysterious lore,
Long was thy prophecy: but if aright
Thou readest all thy fate, how, thus unscared,
Dost thou approach the altar of thy doom,
As fronts the knife some victim, heaven-controlled?

Cassandra:

Friends, there is no avoidance in delay.

Chorus:

Yet who delays the longest, his the gain.

Cassandra:

The day is come--flight were small gain to me!

Chorus:

O brave endurance of a soul resolved!

Cassandra:

That were ill praise, for those of happier doom.

Chorus:

All fame is happy, even famous death.

Cassandra:

Ah sire, ah brethren, famous once were ye!

She moves to enter the house, then starts back.

Chorus:

What fear is this that scares thee from the house?

Cassandra:

Pah!

Chorus:

What is this cry? some dark despair of soul?

Cassandra:

Pah! the house fumes with stench and spilth of blood.

Chorus:

How? 'tis the smell of household offerings.

Cassandra:

'Tis rank as charnel-scent from open graves.

Chorus:

Thou canst not mean this scented Syrian nard?

Cassandra:

Nay, let me pass within to cry aloud
The monarch's fate and mine--enough of life.
Ah friends!
Bear to me witness, since I fall in death,
That not as birds that shun the bush and scream
I moan in idle terror. This attest
When for my death's revenge another dies,
A woman for a woman, and a man
Falls, for a man ill-wedded to his curse.
Grant me this boon--the last before I die.

Chorus:

Brave to the last! I mourn thy doom foreseen.

Cassandra:

Once more one utterance, but not of wail,
Though for my death--and then I speak no more.

I thou whose beam I shall not see again,
To thee I cry, Let those whom vengeance calls
To slay their kindred's slayers, quit withal
The death of me, the slave, the fenceless prey.

Ah state of mortal man! in time of weal,
A line, a shadow! and if ill fate fall,
One wet sponge-sweep wipes all our trace away--
And this I deem less piteous, of the twain.

Exit into the palace.

Chorus:

Too true it is! our mortal state
With bliss is never satiate,
And none, before the palace high
And stately of prosperity,
Cries to us with a voice of fear,
"Away! 'tis ill to enter here!"

Lo! this our lord hath trodden down,
By grace of heaven, old Priam's town,
And praised as god he stands once more
On Argos' shore!
Yet now--if blood shed long ago
Cries out that other blood shall flow--
His life-blood, his, to pay again
The stern requital of the slain--
Peace to that braggart's vaunting vain,
Who, having heard the chieftain's tale,
Yet boasts of bliss untouched by bale!

A loud cry from within.
Voice of Agamemnon:

O I am sped--a deep, a mortal blow.

Chorus:

Listen, listen! who is screaming as in mortal agony?

Voice of Agamemnon:

O! O! again, another, another blow!

Chorus:

The bloody act is over--I have heard the monarch cry--
Let us swiftly take some counsel, lest we too be doomed to die.

One of the Chorus:

'Tis best, I judge, aloud for aid to call,
Ho! loyal Argives! to the palace, all!

Another:

Better, I deem, ourselves to bear the aid,
And drag the deed to light, while drips the blade.

Another:

Such will is mine, and what thou say'st I say:
Swiftly to act! the time brooks no delay.

Another:

Ay, for 'tis plain, this prelude of their song
Foretells its close in tyranny and wrong.

Another:

Behold, we tarry--but thy name, Delay,
They spurn, and press with sleepless hand to slay.

Another:

I know not what 'twere well to counsel now--
Who wills to act, 'tis his to counsel how.

Another:

Thy doubt is mine: for when a man is slain,
I have no words to bring his life again.

Another:

What? e'en for life's sake, bow us to obey
These house-defilers and their tyrant sway?

Another:

Unmanly doom! 'twere better far to die--
Death is a gentler lord than tyranny.

Another:

Think well--must cry or sign of woe or pain
Fix our conclusion that the chief is slain?

Another:

Such talk befits us when the deed we see--
Conjecture dwells afar from certainty.

Leader of the Chorus:

I read one will from many a diverse word,
To know aright, how stands it with our lord!

The scene opens, disclosing Clytemnestra, who comes forward.
The body of Agamemnon lies, muffled in a long robe, within a
silver-sided laver; the corpse of Cassandra is laid beside him.

Clytemnestra:

Ho, ye who heard me speak so long and oft
The glozing word that led me to my will?
Hear how I shrink not to unsay it all!
How else should one who willeth to requite
Evil for evil to an enemy
Disguised as friend, weave the mesh straitly round him,
Not to be overleaped, a net of doom?
This is the sum and issue of old strife,
Of me deep-pondered and at length fulfilled.
All is avowed, and as I smote I stand
With foot set firm upon a finished thing!
I turn not to denial: thus I wrought
So that he could nor flee nor ward his doom,
Even as the trammel hems the scaly shoal,
I trapped him with inextricable toils,
The ill abundance of a baffling robe;
Then smote him, once, again--and at each wound
He cried aloud, then as in death relaxed
Each limb and sank to earth; and as he lay,
Once more I smote him, with the last third blow,
Sacred to Hades, saviour of the dead.
And thus he fell, and as he passed away,
Spirit with body chafed; each dying breath
Flung from his breast swift bubbling jets of gore,
And the dark sprinklings of the rain of blood
Fell upon me; and I was fain to feel
That dew--not sweeter is the rain of heaven
To cornland, when the green sheath teems with grain,

Elders of Argos--since the thing stands so,
I bid you to rejoice, if such your will:
Rejoice or not, I vaunt and praise the deed,
And well I ween, if seemly it could be,
'Twere not ill done to pour libations here,
Justly--ay, more than justly--on his corpse
Who filled his home with curses as with wine,
And thus returned to drain the cup he filled.

Chorus:

I marvel at thy tongue's audacity,
To vaunt thus loudly o'er a husband slain.

Clytemnestra:

Ye hold me as a woman, weak of will,
And strive to sway me: but my heart is stout,
Nor fears to speak its uttermost to you,
Albeit ye know its message. Praise or blame,
Even as ye list,--I reck not of your words.
Lo! at my feet lies Agamemnon slain,
My husband once--and him this hand of mine,
A right contriver, fashioned for his death.
Behold the deed!

Chorus:

Woman, what deadly birth,
What venomed essence of the earth
Or dark distilment of the wave,
To thee such passion gave,
Nerving thine hand
To set upon thy brow this burning crown,
The curses of thy land?
"Our king by thee cut off, hewn down!
Go forth--they cry--accursèd and forlorn,
To hate and scorn!"

Clytemnestra:

O ye just men, who speak my sentence now,
The city's hate, the ban of all my realm!
Ye had no voice of old to launch such doom
On him, my husband, when he held as light
My daughter's life as that of sheep or goat,
One victim from the thronging fleecy fold!
Yea, slew in sacrifice his child and mine,

The well-loved issue of my travail-pangs,
To lull and lay the gales that blew from Thrace.
That deed of his, I say, that stain and shame,
Had rightly been atoned by banishment;
But ye, who then were dumb, are stern to judge
This deed of mine that doth affront your ears.
Storm out your threats, yet knowing this for sooth,
That I am ready, if your hand prevail
As mine now doth, to bow beneath your sway:
If God say nay, it shall be yours to learn
By chastisement a late humility.

Chorus:

Bold is thy craft, and proud
Thy confidence, thy vaunting loud;
Thy soul, that chose a murd'ress' fate,
Is all with blood elate--
Maddened to know
The blood not yet avenged, the damnèd spot
Crimson upon thy brow.
But Fate prepares for thee thy lot--
Smitten as thou didst smite, without a friend,
To meet thine end!

Clytemnestra:

Hear then the sanction of the oath I swear?
By the great vengeance for my murdered child,
By Atè, by the Fury unto whom
This man lies sacrificed by hand of mine,
I do not look to tread the hall of Fear,
While in this hearth and home of mine there burns
The light of love--Aegisthus--as of old
Loyal, a stalwart shield of confidence--
As true to me as this slain man was false,
Wronging his wife with paramours at Troy,
Fresh from the kiss of each Chryseis there!
Behold him dead--behold his captive prize,

Seeress and harlot--comfort of his bed,
True prophetess, true paramour--I wot
The sea-bench was not closer to the flesh,
Full oft, of every rower, than was she.
See, ill they did, and ill requites them now.
His death ye know: she as a dying swan
Sang her last dirge, and lies, as erst she lay,
Close to his side, and to my couch has left
A sweet new taste of joys that know no fear.

Chorus:

Ah woe and well-a-day! I would that Fate--
Not bearing agony too great,
Nor stretching me too long on couch of pain--
Would bid mine eyelids keep
The morningless and unawakening sleep!
For life is weary, now my lord is slain,
The gracious among kings!
Hard fate of old he bore and many grievous things,
And for a woman's sake, on Ilian land--
Now is his life hewn down, and by a woman's hand.
O Helen, O infatuate soul,
Who bad'st the tides of battle roll,
Overwhelming thousands, life on life,
Neath Ilion's wall!
And now lies dead the lord of all.
The blossom of thy storied sin
Bears blood's inexpiable stain,
O thou that erst, these halls within,
Wert unto all a rock of strife,
A husband's bane!

Clytemnestra:

Peace! pray not thou for death as though
Thine heart was whelmed beneath this woe,
Nor turn thy wrath aside to ban
The name of Helen, nor recall

How she, one bane of many a man,
Sent down to death the Danaan lords,
To sleep at Troy the sleep of swords,
And wrought the woe that shattered all.

Chorus:

Fiend of the race! that swoopest fell
Upon the double stock of Tantalus,
Lording it o'er me by a woman's will,
Stern, manful, and imperious?
A bitter sway to me!
Thy very form I see,
Like some grim raven, perched upon the slain,
Exulting o'er the crime, aloud, in tuneless strain!

Clytemnestra:

Right was that word--thou namest well
The brooding race-fiend, triply fell!
From him it is that murder's thirst,
Blood-lapping, inwardly is nursed--
Ere time the ancient scar can sain,
New blood comes welling forth again.

Chorus:

Grim is his wrath and heavy on our home,
That fiend of whom thy voice has cried,
Alas, an omened cry of woe unsatisfied,
An all-devouring doom!

Ah woe, ah Zeus! from Zeus all things befall--
Zeus the high cause and finisher of all!--
Lord of our mortal state, by him are willed
All things, by him fulfilled!

Yet ah my king, my king no more!
What words to say, what tears to pour

Can tell my love for thee?
The spider-web of treachery
She wove and wound, thy life around,
And lo! I see thee lie,
And thro' a coward, impious wound
Pant forth thy life and die!
A death of shame--ah woe on woe!
A treach'rous hand, a cleaving blow!

Clytemnestra:

My guilt thou harpest, o'er and o'er!
I bid thee reckon me no more
As Agamemnon's spouse.
The old Avenger, stern of mood
For Atreus and his feast of blood,
Hath struck the lord of Atreus' house,
And in the semblance of his wife
The king hath slain.--
Yea, for the murdered children's life,
A chieftain's in requital ta'en.

Chorus:

Thou guiltless of this murder, thou!
Who dares such thought avow?
Yet it may be, wroth for the parent's deed,
The fiend hath holpen thee to slay the son.
Dark Ares, god of death, is pressing on
Thro' streams of blood by kindred shed,
Exacting the accompt for children dead,
For clotted blood, for flesh on which their sire did feed.

Yet ah my king, my king no more!
What words to say, what tears to pour
Can tell my love for thee?
The spider-web of treachery
She wove and wound, thy life around,
And lo! I see thee lie,

And thro' a coward, impious wound
Pant forth thy life and die!
A death of shame--ah woe on woe!
A treach'rous hand, a cleaving blow!

Clytemnestra:

I deem not that the death he died
Had overmuch of shame:
For this was he who did provide
Foul wrong unto his house and name:
His daughter, blossom of my womb,
He gave unto a deadly doom,
Iphigenia, child of tears!
And as he wrought, even so he fares.
Nor be his vaunt too loud in hell;
For by the sword his sin he wrought,
And by the sword himself is brought
Among the dead to dwell.

Chorus:

Ah whither shall I fly?
For all in ruin sinks the kingly hall;
Nor swift device nor shift of thought have I,
To 'scape its fall.
A little while the gentler rain-drops fail;
I stand distraught--a ghastly interval,
Till on the roof-tree rings the bursting hail
Of blood and doom. Even now fate whets the steel
On whetstones new and deadlier than of old,
The steel that smites, in Justice' hold,
Another death to deal.
O Earth! that I had lain at rest
And lapped for ever in thy breast,
Ere I had seen my chieftain fall
Within the laver's silver wall,
Low-lying on dishonoured bier!
And who shall give him sepulchre,

And who the wail of sorrow pour?
Woman, 'tis thine no more!
A graceless gift unto his shade
Such tribute, by his murd'ress paid!
Strive not thus wrongly to atone
The impious deed thy hand hath done.
Ah who above the god-like chief
Shall weep the tears of loyal grief?
Who speak above his lowly grave
The last sad praises of the brave?

Clytemnestra:

Peace! for such task is none of thine.
By me he fell, by me he died,
And now his burial rites be mine!
Yet from these halls no mourners' train
Shall celebrate his obsequies;
Only by Acheron's rolling tide
His child shall spring unto his side,
And in a daughter's loving wise
Shall clasp and kiss him once again!

Chorus:

Lo! sin by sin and sorrow dogg'd by sorrow--
And who the end can know?
The slayer of to-day shall die to-morrow--
The wage of wrong is woe.
While Time shall be, while Zeus in heaven is lord,
His law is fixed and stern;
On him that wrought shall vengeance be outpoured--
The tides of doom return.
The children of the curse abide within
These halls of high estate--
And none can wrench from off the home of sin
The clinging grasp of fate.

Clytemnestra:

Now walks thy word aright, to tell
This ancient truth of oracle;
But I with vows of sooth will pray
To him, the power that holdeth sway
O'er all the race of Pleisthenes--
"Tho' dark the deed and deep the guilt,
With this last blood, my hands have spilt,
I pray thee let thine anger cease!
I pray thee pass from us away
To some new race in other lands,
There, if than wilt, to wrong and slay
The lives of men by kindred hands."

For me 'tis all sufficient meed,
Tho' little wealth or power were won,
So I can say, "'Tis past and done.
The bloody lust and murderous,
The inborn frenzy of our house,
Is ended, by my deed!"

Enter Aegisthus.

Aegisthus:

Dawn of the day of rightful vengeance, hail!
I dare at length aver that gods above
Have care of men and heed of earthly wrongs.
I, I who stand and thus exult to see
This man lie wound in robes the Furies wove,
Slain in requital of his father's craft.
Take ye the truth, that Atreus, this man's sire,
The lord and monarch of this land of old,
Held with my sire Thyestes deep dispute,
Brother with brother, for the prize of sway,
And drave him from his home to banishment.
Thereafter, the lorn exile homeward stole
And clung a suppliant to the hearth divine,
And for himself won this immunity?

Not with his own blood to defile the land
That gave him birth. But Atreus, godless sire
Of him who here lies dead, this welcome planned--
With zeal that was not love he feigned to hold
In loyal joy a day of festal cheer,
And bade my father to his board, and set
Before him flesh that was his children once.
First, sitting at the upper board alone,
He hid the fingers and the feet, but gave
The rest--and readily Thyestes took
What to his ignorance no semblance wore
Of human flesh, and ate: behold what curse
That eating brought upon our race and name!
For when he knew what all unhallowed thing
He thus had wrought, with horror's bitter cry
Back-starting, spewing forth the fragments foul,
On Pelops' house a deadly curse he spake?
"As darkly as I spurn this damned food,
So perish all the race of Pleisthenes!"
Thus by that curse fell he whom here ye see,
And I--who else?--this murder wove and planned;
For me, an infant yet in swaddling bands,
Of the three children youngest, Atreus sent
To banishment by my sad father's side:
But Justice brought me home once more, grown now
To manhood's years; and stranger tho' I was,
My right hand reached unto the chieftain's life,
Plotting and planning all that malice bade.
And death itself were honour now to me,
Beholding him in Justice' ambush ta'en.

Chorus:
Aegisthus, for this insolence of thine
That vaunts itself in evil, take my scorn.
Of thine own will, thou sayest, thou hast slain
The chieftain, by thine own unaided plot
Devised the piteous death: I rede thee well,
Think not thy head shall 'scape, when right prevails,
The people's ban, the stones of death and doom.

Aegisthus:

This word from thee, this word from one who rows
Low at the oars beneath, what time we rule,
We of the upper tier? Thou'lt know anon,
'Tis bitter to be taught again in age,
By one so young, submission at the word.
But iron of the chain and hunger's throes
Can minister unto an o'erswoln pride
Marvellous well, ay, even in the old.
Hast eyes, and seest not this? Peace--kick not thus
Against the pricks, unto thy proper pain!

Chorus:

Thou womanish man, waiting till war did cease,
Home-watcher and defiler of the couch,
And arch-deviser of the chieftain's doom!

Aegisthus:

Bold words again! but they shall end in tears.
The very converse, thine, of Orpheus' tongue:
He roused and led in ecstasy of joy
All things that heard his voice melodious;
But thou as with the futile cry of curs
Wilt draw men wrathfully upon thee. Peace!
Or strong subjection soon shall tame thy tongue.

Chorus:

Ay, thou art one to hold an Argive down--
Thou, skilled to plan the murder of the king,
But not with thine own hand to smite the blow!

Aegisthus:

That fraudful force was woman's very part,

Not mine, whom deep suspicion from of old
Would have debarred. Now by his treasure's aid
My purpose holds to rule the citizens.
But whoso will not bear my guiding hand,
Him for his corn-fed mettle I will drive
Not as a trace-horse, light-caparisoned,
But to the shafts with heaviest harness bound.
Famine, the grim mate of the dungeon dark,
Shall look on him and shall behold him tame.

Chorus:

Thou losel soul, was then thy strength too slight
To deal in murder, while a woman's hand,
Staining and shaming Argos and its gods,
Availed to slay him? Ho, if anywhere
The light of life smite on Orestes' eyes,
Let him, returning by some guardian fate,
Hew down with force her paramour and her!

Aegisthus:

How thy word and act shall issue, thou shalt shortly understand.

Chorus:

Up to action, O my comrades! for the fight is hard at hand
Swift, your right hands to the sword hilt! bare the weapon as for
strife--

Aegisthus:

Lo! I too am standing ready, hand on hilt for death or life.

Chorus:

'Twas thy word and we accept it: onward to the chance of war!

Clytemnestra:

Nay, enough, enough, my champion! we will smite and slay
no more.
Already have we reaped enough the harvest-field of guilt:
Enough of wrong and murder, let no other blood be spilt.
Peace, old men! and pass away unto the homes by Fate decreed,
Lest ill valour meet our vengeance--'twas a necessary deed.
But enough of toils and troubles--be the end, if ever, now,
Ere thy talon, O Avenger, deal another deadly blow.
Tis a woman's word of warning, and let who willlist thereto.

Aegisthus:

But that these should loose and lavish reckless blossoms of the tongue,
And in hazard of their fortune cast upon me words of wrong,

And forget the law of subjects, and revile theirruler's word--

Chorus:

Ruler? but 'tis not for Argives, thus to own a dastard lord!

Aegisthus:

I will follow to chastise thee in my coming days of sway.

Chorus:

Not if Fortune guide Orestes safely on his homeward way.

Aegisthus:

Ah, well I know how exiles feed on hopes of their return.

Chorus:

Fare and batten on pollution of the right, while 'tis thy turn.

Aegisthus:

Thou shalt pay, be well assured, heavy quittance for thy pride

Chorus:

Crow and strut, with her to watch thee, like a cock, his mate beside!

Clytemnestra:

Heed not thou too highly of them--let the cur-pack growl and yell:
I and thou will rule the palace and will order all things well.

Exeunt.

Made in the USA
Lexington, KY
15 August 2016